THE COLLEGE SEARCH ORGANIZER

PETER PAUPER PRESS, INC.
WHITE PLAINS, NEW YORK

PETER PAUPER PRESS
Fine Books and Gifts Since 1928

Our Company

In 1928, at the age of twenty-two, Peter Beilenson began printing books on a small press in the basement of his parents' home in Larchmont, New York. Peter—and later, his wife, Edna—sought to create fine books that sold at "prices even a pauper could afford."

Today, still family owned and operated, Peter Pauper Press continues to honor our founders' legacy—and our customers' expectations—of beauty, quality, and value.

——

Illustrations copyright © Mike McDonald
and Curly Pat, used under license from Shutterstock.com

Designed by Margaret Rubiano

Copyright © 2016
Published by
Peter Pauper Press, Inc.
202 Mamaroneck Avenue
White Plains, NY 10601
All rights reserved
ISBN 978-1-4413-1935-7
Printed in China
7 6 5 4 3 2 1

Visit us at www.peterpauper.com

TABLE OF CONTENTS

INTRODUCTION

The College Search Organizer is intended to help guide you through the process of selecting a college. This organizer will assist you in evaluating your strengths and preferences, and serve as a quick reference to keep track of your test scores and other relevant data as you visit various schools. Valuable tools include:

- *The essential timeline and checklist for the college search process*

- *A chart to record test scores*

- *Places to track scholarship applications*

- *A fill-in chart for comparing features of your top college contenders*

- *Guided note-taking pages to track applications and responses, and record notes from college visits*

Use this organizer to know what to do when, collect your thoughts as you visit schools and gather vital information, and prioritize your preferences as you compare schools. This handy book is a convenient way to categorize and simplify the process of obtaining that coveted acceptance letter!

TIMELINE

Task

Complete? (Check) ☐

SELF-EVALUATION

When: Anytime. Self-evaluation can begin as early as eighth grade. This stage of the college search entails taking into consideration what interests you, what types of careers you wish to pursue, and what you're looking for in a college.

COLLEGE RESEARCH ☐

When: Anytime. Begin research as soon as possible into which schools to consider. Visit college websites, talk to representatives at college fairs, or ask alumni or current students for information. Focus on schools that sound like they specialize in your interests, and don't be afraid of schools you haven't heard of.

COLLEGE VISITS ☐

When: Anytime. Like self-evaluation, you can begin to visit colleges anytime. Visit colleges whenever you go on vacation. Want to stay close to home for school? Visit local colleges on the weekend. Guided college tours take roughly one to two hours depending on the size of the campus, but plan for at least half a day to get the full college experience.

ESTABLISH COLLEGE BUDGET ☐

When: Anytime. While saving for college should begin in a student's childhood, it frequently helps to draw up a budget in order to gauge how much you'd need to cover the cost of tuition, room, board, books, transportation, supplies, and other expenses. Do this as early as possible as well to understand your price range when it comes to shopping for colleges.

JOIN SCHOOL ACTIVITIES ☐

When: Ninth Grade. Joining school activities (including sports, clubs, bands, and theater productions) can boost your chances of being noticed by admissions boards, especially if you participate in a wide variety of activities, or activities that show a high interest in a particular field. Admissions boards are attracted to well-rounded people, not simply people who achieve a 4.0 GPA.

PARTICIPATE IN OFF-CAMPUS ACTIVITIES ☐

When: Ninth Grade. Volunteer work, internships, part-time jobs, sports leagues outside of school, and other activities pursued beyond school grounds can pad out high school resumes, particularly if your high school doesn't offer a wide selection of clubs.

TALK TO A COUNSELOR ☐

When: Ninth Grade. Talking to a guidance counselor early not only allows you to establish a relationship with the person safeguarding student transcripts, but it also gives you the opportunity to get advice on the best courses to take between freshman year and the college application process.

TALK TO YOUR TEACHERS ☐

When: Ninth Grade. Students, get used to talking to your teachers and getting to know them during high school. At some point when it comes time to ask for a letter of recommendation, you'll have a list of people to choose from who will vouch for you. Not only that, but also, most college professors will encourage you to ask questions during and after class, so it's just good practice.

TAKE THE PSAT/PLAN ☐

When: Tenth Grade. Applying for colleges in the United States? Then you'll have to start thinking about the SAT and the ACT. The PSAT and PLAN, pretests for the SAT and ACT respectively, are technically optional, but they help students gain an understanding of what taking the real exams is like. This insight will be essential for studying and preparing for the actual SAT or ACT. Additionally, students who score well on the PSAT may qualify for scholarships via the National Merit Scholarship Program.

TAKE THE SAT/ACT ☐

When: Eleventh Grade. As tempting as it may be because of the multiple administration dates, never leave your exams for the last minute. Take them early so you have one less thing to worry about, or so you can retake them later if necessary. Which test is best for you? If you're stronger with reading comprehension and writing, take the SAT. If you're more comfortable with math, science, and logical reasoning, take the ACT.

SCHOLARSHIP SEARCH ☐

When: Eleventh Grade. There's a scholarship for everything these days, and every little bit helps. Think hard about your background and what you wrote down on your self-evaluation sheet as you continue to search and apply for scholarships.

SUBMIT COLLEGE APPLICATIONS ☐

When: Twelfth Grade, Summer/Autumn. The sooner you get started on your applications, the easier this step will be. Fill out a bit of your applications each day, rather than attempt to complete an entire application in one sitting. At this stage, you can also consider applying for early decision if you have your heart set on a particular school.

DRAFT COLLEGE ESSAYS □

When: Twelfth Grade, Summer/Autumn. Most colleges will ask you to write an essay based on a prompt they include with the application. This essay isn't for you to prove your writing skills; it's your chance to demonstrate to an admissions board that you are the passionate student they want at their school. So take your time, plan your essay, write more than one draft, and proofread!

SUBMIT COLLEGE SUPPLEMENTS □

When: Twelfth Grade, Summer/Autumn. Some schools also require a college supplement, an extra application, or additional material such as a portfolio. Read over your college admission requirements to see if your schools ask for anything beyond a single application.

SUBMIT TRANSCRIPT □

When: Twelfth Grade, Autumn/Winter. Speak with your guidance counselor to send your current transcript to your colleges of choice.

OBTAIN LETTERS OF RECOMMENDATION □

When: Twelfth Grade, Autumn/Winter. Most colleges will require at least two letters of recommendation. It's best to ask more than two teachers for recommendations so that you're sure to get letters crafted specifically for each college admissions board, rather than a generic form letter. Also, request these from the teachers with whom you have connected the most. Favorite teachers or teachers for classes where you have excelled are your best bets.

COMPLETE THE FAFSA □

When: Twelfth Grade, Winter. Need financial aid? Then the FAFSA (Free Application for Federal Student Aid) is essential. The FAFSA, sponsored by the Department of Education, is an in-depth report on the financial situation of the student and their families, and it's used to determine how much federal aid each student qualifies for. Many colleges use the FAFSA reports to allocate financial aid. Be aware that when you file your FAFSA, you will be asked to provide a lot of information, including numbers (estimated or actual) from the upcoming year's taxes.

SUBMIT COLLEGE ACCEPTANCE MATERIALS □

When: Twelfth Grade, Spring. Think the moment you have your acceptance letter in-hand, that's the end of that? Nope! Upon receiving your decision, the college you've chosen to attend will send you an admissions packet, which is not so much a congratulations as it is additional paperwork to fill out. These packets include everything from housing request forms to required immunization forms. Read over everything you receive and follow each step carefully to ensure that your transition into college goes smoothly.

SELF-EVALUATION

Knowing your strengths, weaknesses, and interests is often the first step to choosing the best college to suit your needs. After all, no two colleges are alike, and one college might excel in turning out engineers while another might be a better fit for future teachers. Before you start your hunt for the perfect college, take a few moments to perform the following self-evaluation.

Interests: ....

....

....

Best subject: ....

Worst subject: ....

Achievements/Awards: ....

....

....

Current activities: ....

....

....

Greatest strengths: ....

....

....

Greatest weaknesses:

• TOP FIVE DREAM JOBS •

• MAJORS OF INTEREST •

COLLEGE PREFERENCES AND CRITERIA

It helps to narrow down your college search to know what you value, what you don't want, if you meet the school's academic criteria, and if the cost of the school (after anticipated aid) is affordable.

I prefer:

☐ A small school   ☐ A large school

☐ An urban setting   ☐ A suburban setting   ☐ A rural setting

☐ Co-ed (if so, optimal gender ratio: _____)   ☐ Single-sex

☐ Large classes   ☐ Small classes

☐ Religious   ☐ Non-denominational

A school with strength in these majors or courses of study: ....

....

Geographic location: ....

Realistic college price tag: ....

Must-have student activities and clubs (Greek life): ....

....

Must-have athletics: ....

....

Admission requirements relative to...

My GPA: _____ My class rank:_____ My SAT scores:_____

TEST SCORES

Name of Test	Date	Score	Score	Score

QUICK COLLEGE COMPARISON CHART

COLLEGE	LOCATION	STUDENT POPULATION	CAMPUS SIZE	GENDER RATIO

QUICK COLLEGE COMPARISON CHART

Student-Faculty Ratio	Typical Class Size	Admission Requirements	Cost	$ Aid

QUICK COLLEGE COMPARISON CHART

College	Location	Student population	Campus size	Gender ratio

QUICK COLLEGE COMPARISON CHART

Student-faculty ratio	Typical class size	Admission requirements	Cost	$ Aid

QUICK CHECKLIST CHART

College	App. deadline/ sent	Visit date	Interview	App./essay due/ sent

QUICK CHECKLIST CHART

Supplement material due/sent	Transcript due/sent	Test scores due/sent	Letters of rec. due/sent	Accepted? $ Aid?

QUICK CHECKLIST CHART

College	App. deadline/ sent	Visit date	Interview	App./essay due/ sent

QUICK CHECKLIST CHART

Supplement material due/ sent	Transcript due/sent	Test scores due/sent	Letters of rec. due/sent	Accepted? $ Aid?

COLLEGE VISITS

SCHOOL NAME .... Date of visit: ....

School location and setting: ....

Notes from information session: ....

....

....

Names of people met: ....

....

Work-study/Internship options: ....

Study abroad programs: ....

Athletics and extracurriculars: ....

Greek life: ....

Do many students go home/leave on the weekends: ....

Residential details—

    Singles or suites available? ....

    On-campus apartments offered? ....

    Co-ed floors/buildings? ....

    Noise-free or substance-free dorms? ....

    Off-campus options? ....

    Is there guaranteed on-campus housing for all four years? ....

Food—

    Dining locations: ....

    Meal plans: ....

Campus safety: ....

Distance to nearest large city: ....

Transportation on and off campus: ....

Nearest airport: .... Train/bus station: ....

Impressions of the school, the campus atmosphere, and the facilities:

Impressions of the area and nearby amenities:

Thoughts on student life (Do I think I would fit in?):

Thoughts on academics, including majors and courses of interest, and core requirements:

Rate this school for me:

★   ★★   ★★★   ★★★★   ★★★★★

0 (not a fit)   Perfect fit!

COLLEGE VISITS

SCHOOL NAME .... Date of visit: ....

School location and setting: ....

Notes from information session: ....

....

....

Names of people met: ....

....

Work-study/Internship options: ....

Study abroad programs: ....

Athletics and extracurriculars: ....

Greek life: ....

Do many students go home/leave on the weekends: ....

Residential details—

    Singles or suites available? ....

    On-campus apartments offered? ....

    Co-ed floors/buildings? ....

    Noise-free or substance-free dorms? ....

    Off-campus options? ....

    Is there guaranteed on-campus housing for all four years? ....

Food—

    Dining locations: ....

    Meal plans: ....

Campus safety: ....

Distance to nearest large city: ....

Transportation on and off campus: ....

Nearest airport: .... Train/bus station: ....

Impressions of the school, the campus atmosphere, and the facilities:

Impressions of the area and nearby amenities:

Thoughts on student life (Do I think I would fit in?):

Thoughts on academics, including majors and courses of interest, and core requirements:

Rate this school for me:

★	★★	★★★	★★★★	★★★★★
0 (not a fit)				Perfect fit!

COLLEGE VISITS

SCHOOL NAME .... Date of visit: ....

School location and setting: ....

Notes from information session: ....
....
....
....

Names of people met: ....
....

Work-study/Internship options: ....

Study abroad programs: ....

Athletics and extracurriculars: ....

Greek life: ....

Do many students go home/leave on the weekends: ....

Residential details—

    Singles or suites available? ....

    On-campus apartments offered? ....

    Co-ed floors/buildings? ....

    Noise-free or substance-free dorms? ....

    Off-campus options? ....

    Is there guaranteed on-campus housing for all four years? ....

Food—

    Dining locations: ....

    Meal plans: ....

Campus safety: ....

Distance to nearest large city: ....

Transportation on and off campus: ....

Nearest airport: .... Train/bus station: ....

Impressions of the school, the campus atmosphere, and the facilities:

Impressions of the area and nearby amenities:

Thoughts on student life (Do I think I would fit in?):

Thoughts on academics, including majors and courses of interest, and core requirements:

Rate this school for me:

★   ★★   ★★★   ★★★★   ★★★★★

0 (not a fit)   Perfect fit!

COLLEGE VISITS

SCHOOL NAME .... Date of visit: ....

School location and setting: ....

Notes from information session: ....

Names of people met: ....

Work-study/Internship options: ....

Study abroad programs: ....

Athletics and extracurriculars: ....

Greek life: ....

Do many students go home/leave on the weekends: ....

Residential details—

    Singles or suites available? ....

    On-campus apartments offered? ....

    Co-ed floors/buildings? ....

    Noise-free or substance-free dorms? ....

    Off-campus options? ....

    Is there guaranteed on-campus housing for all four years? ....

Food—

    Dining locations: ....

    Meal plans: ....

Campus safety: ....

Distance to nearest large city: ....

Transportation on and off campus: ....

Nearest airport: .... Train/bus station: ....

Impressions of the school, the campus atmosphere, and the facilities:

Impressions of the area and nearby amenities:

Thoughts on student life (Do I think I would fit in?):

Thoughts on academics, including majors and courses of interest, and core requirements:

Rate this school for me:

★   ★★   ★★★   ★★★★   ★★★★★
0 (not a fit)   Perfect fit!

COLLEGE VISITS

SCHOOL NAME .... Date of visit: ....

School location and setting: ....

Notes from information session: ....

....

....

Names of people met: ....

....

Work-study/Internship options: ....

Study abroad programs: ....

Athletics and extracurriculars: ....

Greek life: ....

Do many students go home/leave on the weekends: ....

Residential details—

    Singles or suites available? ....

    On-campus apartments offered? ....

    Co-ed floors/buildings? ....

    Noise-free or substance-free dorms? ....

    Off-campus options? ....

    Is there guaranteed on-campus housing for all four years? ...

Food—

    Dining locations: ....

    Meal plans: ....

Campus safety: ....

Distance to nearest large city: ....

Transportation on and off campus: ....

Nearest airport: .... Train/bus station: ....

Impressions of the school, the campus atmosphere, and the facilities:

Impressions of the area and nearby amenities:

Thoughts on student life (Do I think I would fit in?):

Thoughts on academics, including majors and courses of interest, and core requirements:

Rate this school for me:

★	★★	★★★	★★★★	★★★★★
0 (not a fit)				Perfect fit!

COLLEGE VISITS

SCHOOL NAME .... Date of visit: ....

School location and setting: ....

Notes from information session: ....

....

....

Names of people met: ....

....

Work-study/Internship options: ....

Study abroad programs: ....

Athletics and extracurriculars: ....

Greek life: ....

Do many students go home/leave on the weekends: ....

Residential details—

    Singles or suites available? ....

    On-campus apartments offered? ....

    Co-ed floors/buildings? ....

    Noise-free or substance-free dorms? ....

    Off-campus options? ....

    Is there guaranteed on-campus housing for all four years? ....

Food—

    Dining locations: ....

    Meal plans: ....

Campus safety: ....

Distance to nearest large city: ....

Transportation on and off campus: ....

Nearest airport: .... Train/bus station: ....

Impressions of the school, the campus atmosphere, and the facilities:

Impressions of the area and nearby amenities:

Thoughts on student life (Do I think I would fit in?):

Thoughts on academics, including majors and courses of interest, and core requirements:

Rate this school for me:

★   ★★   ★★★   ★★★★   ★★★★★
0 (not a fit)   Perfect fit!

COLLEGE VISITS

SCHOOL NAME .... Date of visit: ....

School location and setting: ....

Notes from information session: ....

....

....

Names of people met: ....

....

Work-study/Internship options: ....

Study abroad programs: ....

Athletics and extracurriculars: ....

Greek life: ....

Do many students go home/leave on the weekends: ....

Residential details—

    Singles or suites available? ....

    On-campus apartments offered? ....

    Co-ed floors/buildings? ....

    Noise-free or substance-free dorms? ....

    Off-campus options? ....

    Is there guaranteed on-campus housing for all four years? ....

Food—

    Dining locations: ....

    Meal plans: ....

Campus safety: ....

Distance to nearest large city: ....

Transportation on and off campus: ....

Nearest airport: .... Train/bus station: ....

Impressions of the school, the campus atmosphere, and the facilities:

Impressions of the area and nearby amenities:

Thoughts on student life (Do I think I would fit in?):

Thoughts on academics, including majors and courses of interest, and core requirements:

Rate this school for me:

★	★★	★★★	★★★★	★★★★★
0 (not a fit)				Perfect fit!

COLLEGE VISITS

SCHOOL NAME .... Date of visit: ....

School location and setting: ....

Notes from information session: ....

....

....

....

Names of people met: ....

....

Work-study/Internship options: ....

Study abroad programs: ....

Athletics and extracurriculars: ....

Greek life: ....

Do many students go home/leave on the weekends: ....

Residential details—

    Singles or suites available? ....

    On-campus apartments offered? ....

    Co-ed floors/buildings? ....

    Noise-free or substance-free dorms? ....

    Off-campus options? ....

    Is there guaranteed on-campus housing for all four years? ....

Food—

    Dining locations: ....

    Meal plans: ....

Campus safety: ....

Distance to nearest large city: ....

Transportation on and off campus: ....

Nearest airport: .... Train/bus station: ....

Impressions of the school, the campus atmosphere, and the facilities:

Impressions of the area and nearby amenities:

Thoughts on student life (Do I think I would fit in?):

Thoughts on academics, including majors and courses of interest, and core requirements:

Rate this school for me:

★   ★★   ★★★   ★★★★   ★★★★★

0 (not a fit)   Perfect fit!

COLLEGE VISITS

SCHOOL NAME .... Date of visit: ....

School location and setting: ....

Notes from information session: ....

....

....

Names of people met: ....

....

Work-study/Internship options: ....

Study abroad programs: ....

Athletics and extracurriculars: ....

Greek life: ....

Do many students go home/leave on the weekends: ....

Residential details—

    Singles or suites available? ....

    On-campus apartments offered? ....

    Co-ed floors/buildings? ....

    Noise-free or substance-free dorms? ....

    Off-campus options? ....

    Is there guaranteed on-campus housing for all four years? ....

Food—

    Dining locations: ....

    Meal plans: ....

Campus safety: ....

Distance to nearest large city: ....

Transportation on and off campus: ....

Nearest airport: .... Train/bus station: ....

Impressions of the school, the campus atmosphere, and the facilities:

Impressions of the area and nearby amenities:

Thoughts on student life (Do I think I would fit in?):

Thoughts on academics, including majors and courses of interest, and core requirements:

Rate this school for me:

★	★★	★★★	★★★★	★★★★★
0 (not a fit)				Perfect fit!

COLLEGE VISITS

SCHOOL NAME .... Date of visit: ....

School location and setting: ....

Notes from information session: ....

....

....

Names of people met: ....

....

Work-study/Internship options: ....

Study abroad programs: ....

Athletics and extracurriculars: ....

Greek life: ....

Do many students go home/leave on the weekends: ....

Residential details—

    Singles or suites available? ....

    On-campus apartments offered? ....

    Co-ed floors/buildings? ....

    Noise-free or substance-free dorms? ....

    Off-campus options? ....

    Is there guaranteed on-campus housing for all four years? ....

Food—

    Dining locations: ....

    Meal plans: ....

Campus safety: ....

Distance to nearest large city: ....

Transportation on and off campus: ....

Nearest airport: .... Train/bus station: ....

Impressions of the school, the campus atmosphere, and the facilities:

Impressions of the area and nearby amenities:

Thoughts on student life (Do I think I would fit in?):

Thoughts on academics, including majors and courses of interest, and core requirements:

Rate this school for me:

★   ★★   ★★★   ★★★★   ★★★★★
0 (not a fit)   Perfect fit!

COLLEGE VISITS

SCHOOL NAME .... Date of visit:...................................

School location and setting: ....

Notes from information session: ....

....

....

Names of people met: ....

....

Work-study/Internship options: ....

Study abroad programs: ....

Athletics and extracurriculars: ....

Greek life: ....

Do many students go home/leave on the weekends: ....

Residential details—

    Singles or suites available? ....

    On-campus apartments offered? ....

    Co-ed floors/buildings? ....

    Noise-free or substance-free dorms? ....

    Off-campus options? ....

    Is there guaranteed on-campus housing for all four years? ....

Food—

    Dining locations: ....

    Meal plans: ....

Campus safety: ....

Distance to nearest large city: ....

Transportation on and off campus: ....

Nearest airport: .... Train/bus station: ....

Impressions of the school, the campus atmosphere, and the facilities:

Impressions of the area and nearby amenities:

Thoughts on student life (Do I think I would fit in?):

Thoughts on academics, including majors and courses of interest, and core requirements:

Rate this school for me:

★   ★★   ★★★   ★★★★   ★★★★★

0 (not a fit)   Perfect fit!

COLLEGE VISITS

SCHOOL NAME .... Date of visit: ....

School location and setting: ....

Notes from information session: ....

....

....

Names of people met: ....

....

Work-study/Internship options: ....

Study abroad programs: ....

Athletics and extracurriculars: ....

Greek life: ....

Do many students go home/leave on the weekends: ....

Residential details—

    Singles or suites available? ....

    On-campus apartments offered? ....

    Co-ed floors/buildings? ....

    Noise-free or substance-free dorms? ....

    Off-campus options? ....

    Is there guaranteed on-campus housing for all four years? ....

Food—

    Dining locations: ....

    Meal plans: ....

Campus safety: ....

Distance to nearest large city: ....

Transportation on and off campus: ....

Nearest airport: .... Train/bus station: ....

Impressions of the school, the campus atmosphere, and the facilities: ....
....
....
....
....

Impressions of the area and nearby amenities: ....
....
....
....
....

Thoughts on student life (Do I think I would fit in?): ....
....
....
....
....

Thoughts on academics, including majors and courses of interest, and core
requirements: ....
....
....
....
....

Rate this school for me:

★   ★★   ★★★   ★★★★   ★★★★★
0 (not a fit)   Perfect fit!

COLLEGE VISITS

SCHOOL NAME .... Date of visit: ....

School location and setting: ....

Notes from information session: ....

....

....

Names of people met: ....

....

Work-study/Internship options: ....

Study abroad programs: ....

Athletics and extracurriculars: ....

Greek life: ....

Do many students go home/leave on the weekends: ....

Residential details—

    Singles or suites available? ....

    On-campus apartments offered? ....

    Co-ed floors/buildings? ....

    Noise-free or substance-free dorms? ....

    Off-campus options? ....

    Is there guaranteed on-campus housing for all four years? ....

Food—

    Dining locations: ....

    Meal plans: ....

Campus safety: ....

Distance to nearest large city: ....

Transportation on and off campus: ....

Nearest airport: .... Train/bus station: ....

Impressions of the school, the campus atmosphere, and the facilities:

Impressions of the area and nearby amenities:

Thoughts on student life (Do I think I would fit in?):

Thoughts on academics, including majors and courses of interest, and core requirements:

Rate this school for me:

★	★★	★★★	★★★★	★★★★★
0 (not a fit)				Perfect fit!

COLLEGE VISITS

SCHOOL NAME .... Date of visit: ....

School location and setting: ....

Notes from information session: ....

....

....

Names of people met: ....

....

Work-study/Internship options: ....

Study abroad programs: ....

Athletics and extracurriculars: ....

Greek life: ....

Do many students go home/leave on the weekends: ....

Residential details—

    Singles or suites available? ....

    On-campus apartments offered? ....

    Co-ed floors/buildings? ....

    Noise-free or substance-free dorms? ....

    Off-campus options? ....

    Is there guaranteed on-campus housing for all four years? ....

Food—

    Dining locations: ....

    Meal plans: ....

Campus safety: ....

Distance to nearest large city: ....

Transportation on and off campus: ....

Nearest airport: .... Train/bus station: ....

Impressions of the school, the campus atmosphere, and the facilities:

Impressions of the area and nearby amenities:

Thoughts on student life (Do I think I would fit in?):

Thoughts on academics, including majors and courses of interest, and core requirements:

Rate this school for me:

★	★★	★★★	★★★★	★★★★★
0 (not a fit)				Perfect fit!

COLLEGE VISITS

SCHOOL NAME .... Date of visit: ....

School location and setting: ....

Notes from information session: ....

....

....

Names of people met: ....

....

Work-study/Internship options: ....

Study abroad programs: ....

Athletics and extracurriculars: ....

Greek life: ....

Do many students go home/leave on the weekends: ....

Residential details—

    Singles or suites available? ....

    On-campus apartments offered? ....

    Co-ed floors/buildings? ....

    Noise-free or substance-free dorms? ....

    Off-campus options? ....

    Is there guaranteed on-campus housing for all four years? ....

Food—

    Dining locations: ....

    Meal plans: ....

Campus safety: ....

Distance to nearest large city: ....

Transportation on and off campus: ....

Nearest airport: .... Train/bus station: ....

Impressions of the school, the campus atmosphere, and the facilities:

Impressions of the area and nearby amenities:

Thoughts on student life (Do I think I would fit in?):

Thoughts on academics, including majors and courses of interest, and core requirements:

Rate this school for me:

★   ★★   ★★★   ★★★★   ★★★★★

0 (not a fit)   Perfect fit!

COLLEGE VISITS

SCHOOL NAME .... Date of visit: ....

School location and setting: ....

Notes from information session: ....

....

....

Names of people met: ....

....

Work-study/Internship options: ....

Study abroad programs: ....

Athletics and extracurriculars: ....

Greek life: ....

Do many students go home/leave on the weekends: ....

Residential details—

    Singles or suites available? ....

    On-campus apartments offered? ....

    Co-ed floors/buildings? ....

    Noise-free or substance-free dorms? ....

    Off-campus options? ....

    Is there guaranteed on-campus housing for all four years? ....

Food—

    Dining locations: ....

    Meal plans: ....

Campus safety: ....

Distance to nearest large city: ....

Transportation on and off campus: ....

Nearest airport: .... Train/bus station: ....

Impressions of the school, the campus atmosphere, and the facilities:

Impressions of the area and nearby amenities:

Thoughts on student life (Do I think I would fit in?):

Thoughts on academics, including majors and courses of interest, and core requirements:

Rate this school for me:

★   ★★   ★★★   ★★★★   ★★★★★
0 (not a fit)   Perfect fit!

COLLEGE VISITS

SCHOOL NAME .... Date of visit: ....

School location and setting: ....

Notes from information session: ....

....

....

Names of people met: ....

....

Work-study/Internship options: ....

Study abroad programs: ....

Athletics and extracurriculars: ....

Greek life: ....

Do many students go home/leave on the weekends: ....

Residential details—

    Singles or suites available? ....

    On-campus apartments offered? ....

    Co-ed floors/buildings? ....

    Noise-free or substance-free dorms? ....

    Off-campus options? ....

    Is there guaranteed on-campus housing for all four years? ....

Food—

    Dining locations: ....

    Meal plans: ....

Campus safety: ....

Distance to nearest large city: ....

Transportation on and off campus: ....

Nearest airport: .... Train/bus station: ....

Impressions of the school, the campus atmosphere, and the facilities:

Impressions of the area and nearby amenities:

Thoughts on student life (Do I think I would fit in?):

Thoughts on academics, including majors and courses of interest, and core requirements:

Rate this school for me:

★	★★	★★★	★★★★	★★★★★
0 (not a fit)				Perfect fit!

COLLEGE VISITS

SCHOOL NAME .... Date of visit: ....

School location and setting: ....

Notes from information session: ....

Names of people met: ....

Work-study/Internship options: ....

Study abroad programs: ....

Athletics and extracurriculars: ....

Greek life: ....

Do many students go home/leave on the weekends: ....

Residential details—

    Singles or suites available? ....

    On-campus apartments offered? ....

    Co-ed floors/buildings? ....

    Noise-free or substance-free dorms? ....

    Off-campus options? ....

    Is there guaranteed on-campus housing for all four years? ....

Food—

    Dining locations: ....

    Meal plans: ....

Campus safety: ....

Distance to nearest large city: ....

Transportation on and off campus: ....

Nearest airport: .... Train/bus station: ....

Impressions of the school, the campus atmosphere, and the facilities:

Impressions of the area and nearby amenities:

Thoughts on student life (Do I think I would fit in?):

Thoughts on academics, including majors and courses of interest, and core requirements:

Rate this school for me:

★	★★	★★★	★★★★	★★★★★
0 (not a fit)				Perfect fit!

COLLEGE VISITS

SCHOOL NAME .... Date of visit: ....

School location and setting: ....

Notes from information session: ....

....

....

Names of people met: ....

....

Work-study/Internship options: ....

Study abroad programs: ....

Athletics and extracurriculars: ....

Greek life: ....

Do many students go home/leave on the weekends: ....

Residential details—

    Singles or suites available? ....

    On-campus apartments offered? ....

    Co-ed floors/buildings? ....

    Noise-free or substance-free dorms? ....

    Off-campus options? ....

    Is there guaranteed on-campus housing for all four years? ......

Food—

    Dining locations: ....

    Meal plans: ....

Campus safety: ....

Distance to nearest large city: ....

Transportation on and off campus: ....

Nearest airport: .... Train/bus station: ....

Impressions of the school, the campus atmosphere, and the facilities:

Impressions of the area and nearby amenities:

Thoughts on student life (Do I think I would fit in?):

Thoughts on academics, including majors and courses of interest, and core requirements:

Rate this school for me:

★   ★★   ★★★   ★★★★   ★★★★★

0 (not a fit)   Perfect fit!

COLLEGE VISITS

SCHOOL NAME ....Date of visit:.........................

School location and setting: ....

Notes from information session: ....

....

....

Names of people met: ....

....

Work-study/Internship options: ....

Study abroad programs: ....

Athletics and extracurriculars: ....

Greek life: ....

Do many students go home/leave on the weekends: ....

Residential details—

    Singles or suites available? ....

    On-campus apartments offered? ....

    Co-ed floors/buildings? ....

    Noise-free or substance-free dorms? ....

    Off-campus options? ....

    Is there guaranteed on-campus housing for all four years? ....

Food—

    Dining locations: ....

    Meal plans: ....

Campus safety: ....

Distance to nearest large city: ....

Transportation on and off campus: ....

Nearest airport: ....Train/bus station: ....

Impressions of the school, the campus atmosphere, and the facilities:

Impressions of the area and nearby amenities:

Thoughts on student life (Do I think I would fit in?):

Thoughts on academics, including majors and courses of interest, and core requirements:

Rate this school for me:

★   ★★   ★★★   ★★★★   ★★★★★

0 (not a fit)   Perfect fit!

SCHOLARSHIPS

Name of scholarship	Requirements

SCHOLARSHIPS

DEADLINE/ SUBMITTED	AMOUNT AWARDED

USEFUL RESOURCES

For more information or for links to exams and tools, check out these websites.

The ACT: www.actstudent.org

College Board, official website of the SAT: www.collegeboard.org

ETS, official website of the TOEFL: www.ets.org

FAFSA on the Web (Note that this is the only place where you can fill out the FAFSA. Ignore any other website that offers to file it for you, especially the ones that do it for a fee.): fafsa.ed.gov

Scholarships.com, scholarship search engine: www.scholarships.com

CollegeNavigator, college search engine sponsored by the U.S. Department of Education: nces.ed.gov/collegenavigator

SchoolFinder.com, a college search engine for schools in Canada: www.schoolfinder.com

College Majors 101, a helpful website to gain insight on how to turn your self-evaluation sheet into a major: www.collegemajors101.com

The Common Application, an online application that can be sent to hundreds of schools: www.commonapp.org

NOTES